WOOD PELLET & SMOKER COOKBOOK

BBQ PRESS

© **Copyright 2020 by BBQ PRESS - All rights reserved.**

This paper is geared towards providing exact and reliable information regarding the topic and issue at hand. The publication is sold with the idea that the publisher is not required to render accounting, officially permitted, or otherwise, qualified services. If advice, legal or professional, is needed, you should seek the advice of a person experienced in the profession.

From a statement of principles that has been accepted and approved equally by a committee of the American Bar Association and a committee of publishers and associations.

It is not legal in any way to reproduce, duplicate, or transmit any part of this document in either electronic or printed media. Recording of this publication is strictly prohibited, and any storage of this document is not permitted except with the written permission of the publisher. All rights reserved.

The information provided herein is stated to be true and consistent, in that any liability, in terms of inattention or otherwise, for any use or misuse of any policy, process, or direction contained within is the sole and total responsibility of the receiving reader. Under no circumstances will any legal liability or fault be held against the publisher for any repair, damage, or monetary loss due to the information contained herein, either directly or indirectly.

The respective authors own all copyrights not held by the publisher.

The information contained herein is offered for informational purposes only and is universal as such. The presentation of the information is without contract or any type of warranty assurance.

Trademarks used are without consent, and publication of the trademark is without permission or endorsement from the trademark owner. All trademarks and brands within this book are for clarification purposes only and are the property of the owners themselves, not affiliated with this document.

DISCLAIMER

The information contained in the Book is for informational purposes only, and in no way constitutes the making of a diagnosis or prescription for treatment.

The information contained in this book is not intended and should not in any way replace the direct relationship doctor-patient or specialist examination.

It is recommended that you always seek the advice of your physician and/or specialists for any reported indication.

CONTENTS

8 — Pineapple Habanero Wings

10 — Awesome Honey Smoked Turkey

12 — Citrus Touched Goose Breast

14 — BBQ Pulled Turkey Sandwiches

16 — Spicy Grilled Chicken with Crunchy Fennel Salad

18 — Guacamole And Chicken Dish

20 — All-Time Favorite Chipotle Wings

22 — Herby Quail

24 — Tequila Lime Roasted Turkey

28 — Grilled Chicken with Banana Peppers

30 — Smoked Up Chicken Wrap

32 — Smoked Butter Chicken

35 — Plum Chicken Pop

37 — Chesapeake Garlic Parmesan Wings

39 — Alderwood Turkey Breast

41 — Sizzling' Buffalo Wings

43 — Sriracha BBQ Chicken

45 — Mesquite Bacon And Maple Chicken

CONTENTS

47 — Grilled Chicken Drumsticks with Savory

47 — Caramel

49 — Bacon Cordon Bleu

51 — Duck Poppers

53 — Spiced Lemon Chicken

55 — Citrus Packed Chicken Meal

57 — Smoked Rosemary Chicken Kebab

59 — Turkey Parmigiana

61 — Roast Duck a L'Orange

63 — Lemon Cornish Chicken Stuffed with Crab Meat

65 — Roasted Tuscan Thighs

67 — Smoked Turkey

69 — Baked Garlic Parmesan Wings

71 — Cajun Patch Cock Chicken

73 — Flattened Mojo Chicken

75 — Peanut Chicken Satay

77 — Pork Recipes

77 — Grilled Carnitas

CONTENTS

80 — Roasted Whole Ham in Apricot Sauce

82 — Awesome Pork Shoulder

84 — Smoked Braided Pork Loin

86 — Pork Burnt Ends

89 — Herbed Prime Rib

91 — Explosive Smoky Bacon

94 — Lovable Pork Belly

96 — Lemon Pepper Pork Tenderloin

98 — Smoked Pork Ribs

Pineapple Habanero Wings

Prep Time: 20 Minutes

Cooking Time: 55 Minutes

Servings: 6 Persons

Ingredients

- For Wings
- 2-4 pounds' chicken wings
- Juice of 2 limes, freshly squeezed Jamaican flavored rub
- For The Pineapple Habanero Sauce
- ½ cup brown sugar
- 3 garlic cloves, minced
- 1 pineapple, cut into spears & grilled until grill marks appear
- ½ yellow pepper, diced
- 1 habanero, seeded & diced
- 1/3 cup white vinegar
- 2 tablespoons softened butter
- Salt to taste

Directions

For Wings

Drizzle the lime juice over the bird wings; make sure that they're nicely covered & then, generously season them with the Jamaican rub; set apart and allow them to marinate for overnight.

For Habanero Sauce

Blend the whole elements collectively in a food processor or blender (don't uploads the butter). Pour the organized mixture right into a sauce pan with the softened butter & let simmer on medium warmness for 10 to 15 mins.

Preheat your pellet smoker in advance to 225 F.

three. Smoke the wings for 40 to 45 mins; cautiously flip & growth the temperature to 350 F.

Cook them till they reflect an inner temperature of somewhere one hundred seventy-five to 180 F.

Remove the pieces from pellet grill & observe the organized sauce on each wing.

Increase your pellet grill's temperature to 450 F and put the portions on the grill again; prepare dinner until the sauce is set, for 5 to 7 extra mins. Serve warm and enjoy.

Nutritional Value

919 Calories, 549 Calories from Fat

61g Total Fat, 23g Saturated Fat

0.8g Trans Fat, 10g Polyunsaturated Fat

22g Monounsaturated Fat, 201mg Cholesterol

946mg Sodium, 560mg Potassium

53g Total Carbohydrates, 1.9g Dietary Fiber, 27g Sugars, 39g Protein

Awesome Honey Smoked Turkey

Serving: 7

Prep Time: 6 minutes

Cook Time: 6 hours

Recommended Wood Type: Hickory Wood

Ingredients

- 1 gallon of hot water
- 1 pound of kosher salt
- 2 quarts of vegetable broth
- 8-ounce jars of honey
- 1 cup of orange juice
- A 7-pound bag of ice cubes
- 15 pounds of the whole turkey with giblets and neck removed
- ¼ cup of vegetable oil
- 1 teaspoon of poultry seasoning
- 1 granny smith apple, cored and cut up into large chunks
- 1 celery stalk, cut into chunks
- 1 small onion, cut into chunks
- 1 orange, quartered

How To

Take your drip pan and add water, cover with aluminum foil. Preheat your Smoker to 225 degrees F

Use water fill water pan halfway through and place it over drip pan. Add wood chips to the side tray

Stretch the skin away from drumsticks as much as possible

Remove the tendons from each leg

Season the drumsticks with salt and pepper and transfer to your smoker rack

Smoker for 1 and a ½ hours

Baste the pops with plum sauce and transfer to Smoker again, a smoker for 30 minutes until the internal temperature reaches 165 degrees Fahrenheit

Allow them to rest for a while

Coat the meat with more sauce and enjoy!

Nutrition Values (Per Serving)

Calories: 222

Fats: 11g

Carbs: 16g

Fiber: 3g

Citrus Touched Goose Breast

Serving: 7

Prep Time: 40 minutes

Cook Time: 6 hours

Recommended Wood Type: Hickory

Ingredients

- ½ a cup of orange juice
- 1/3 cup of olive oil
- 1/3 cup of Dijon mustard
- 1/3 cup of brown sugar
- ¼ cup of soy sauce
- ¼ cup of honey
- 1 tablespoon of onion, minced
- 1 teaspoon of garlic powder
- 8 goose breasts, halved

How To

Take a medium-sized bowl and a whisk in orange juice, olive oil, mustard, soy sauce, sugar, honey, onion, garlic powder

Mix well and prepare the marinade

Transfer the goose breast to the marinade and cover

Allow it to refrigerate for 3-6 hours

Take your drip pan and add water, cover with aluminum foil. Preheat your Smoker to 300 degrees F

Use water fill water pan halfway through and place it over drip pan. Add wood chips to the side tray

Transfer the breast to your smoker grate and brush smoke for 6 hours, making sure to keep brushing it with the marinade for the first 30 minutes

Keep Smoking until the internal temperature reaches 165 degrees Fahrenheit

Serve and enjoy!

Nutrition Values (Per Serving)

Calories: 1094

Fats: 64g

Carbs: 14g

Fiber: 13g

BBQ Pulled Turkey Sandwiches

Preparation time: 15 minutes

Cooking time: 1 hour

Servings: 6

Ingredients:

- 6 skin-on turkey thighs
- 6 split and buttered buns
- 1 ½ cups of chicken broth
- 1 cup of BBQ sauce
- Poultry rub
- Intolerances:
- Gluten-Free
- Egg-Free

Directions:

Season the turkey thighs on both sides with poultry rub.

Set the grill to preheat by pushing the temperature to 180°F.

Arrange the turkey thighs on the grate of the grill and smoke it for 30 minutes.

Transfer the thighs to an aluminum foil which is disposable and then pour the brine right around the thighs. Cover it with a lid.

Increase the grill temperature to 325°F and roast the thigh till the internal temperature reaches 180°F.

Remove the foil from the grill, but do not turn off the grill. Let the turkey thighs cool down a little.

Pour the dripping and serve. Remove the skin and discard it.

Pull the meat into shreds and return it to the foil.

Add 1 more cup of BBQ sauce and some more dripping.

Cover the foil with lid and re-heat the turkey on the smoker for half an hour.

Serve and enjoy.

Nutrition:

Calories: 289

Fat: 10g

Cholesterol: 80mg

Carbs: 23g

Protein: 26g

Spicy Grilled Chicken with Crunchy Fennel Salad

Ingredients

- Chicken
- 1½ lb. skinless, boneless chicken thighs
- Kosher salt
- 2 garlic cloves
- 3 oil-packed anchovy fillets (optional)
- 1 red chili (Fresno or Holland), seeds removed and coarsely chopped
- 2 tbsps. of tomato paste
- 2 tsp finely chopped oregano
- 3 tbsps. of extra virgin olive oil, plus more for the grilling
- 2 halved lemons
- Fennel Salad and Assembly
- 2 medium fennel bulbs, outer layers removed, halved lengthwise and thinly sliced
- 1 small white onion, thinly sliced into rounds
- 2 tbsps. unseasoned rice vinegar
- 2 tbsp. of extra virgin olive oil
- Kosher salt
- 1 tbsp. toasted sesame seeds

Recipe Preparation

Chicken

Pat the hen dry and season with salt, then put apart.

Smash the garlic the use of a knife on a cutting board. Add the anchovies, if the usage of, the chili and one or two of pinches of salt and hold mashing together with your knife till paste forms. (You may do this with a mortar and pestle.) Transfer the paste into a large bowl and add in the oregano and three tbsp. of oil. Add the hen and permit it take a seat for at least one hour.

Set up the grill for medium warmness. Clean and oil the grate. Grill the hen, turning once, till lightly burned and cooked through, about four minutes for every facet.

In the meantime, grill the lemons, cut side down, until gently burned and beginning to caramelize- approximately 4 mins. Move onto a platter.

Put the fowl onto the platter with lemons and let it rest for five mins.

Fennel dish and Assembly

While the chook is resting, toss the fennel, onion, and vinegar in a medium bowl, drizzle with oil and season with salt.

Place the fennel salad at the dish subsequent to the chicken and sprinkle with sesame seeds. Squeeze the grilled lemons over the bird and fennel salad.

Guacamole And Chicken Dish

Serving: 4

Prep Time: 10-15 minutes

Cook Time: 1 hour

Recommended Wood Type: Maple Wood

Ingredients

- 2 chicken breasts
- 2 avocado, ripe
- 1 tomato, diced
- 1 lime
- 1 teaspoon salt
- 1 teaspoon garlic powder
- 1 teaspoon Cajun
- Four multigrain bread, slices

How To

Take your drip pan and add water, cover with aluminum foil. Preheat your Smoker to 225 degrees F

Apply Cajun seasoning generously to your chicken breasts

Use water fill water pan halfway through and place it over drip pan. Add wood chips to the side tray.

Add chicken inside your Smoker and Smoke for 1 and ½ hours until internal temperature reaches 165 degrees F

Once done, remove chicken and keep it on the side, let it rest for 10 minutes. Slice up

Cut into avocado into halves and remove seeds, scoop out the flesh into a medium-sized bowl

Squeeze half lemon into the avocado and mix we, spoon to remove all lumps and bring to a smooth mix

Add in chopped tomatoes and onions and stir

Pour rest of the lime juice over avocado mix and season with salt and pepper

Take a slice of multigrain and place chicken and salad mix on top, top with another slice, and enjoy!

Nutrition Values (Per Serving)

Calories: 390

Fat: 27g

Carbohydrates: 32g

Protein: 43g

All-Time Favorite Chipotle Wings

Serving: 8

Prep Time: 75 minutes

Cook Time: 1-2 hours

Recommended Wood Type: Oak Wood

Ingredients

- 2 tablespoon packed light brown sugar
- 1 and a ½ tablespoon of chipotle pepper
- 1 tablespoon of Hungarian smoked paprika
- 1 tablespoon of dry mustard
- 1 tablespoon of ground cumin
- 1 and a ½ teaspoon of salt
- 5 and a ½ pound of chicken wings

How To

Take your drip pan and add water, cover with aluminum foil. Preheat your Smoker to 225 degrees F

Use water fill water pan halfway through and place it over drip pan. Add wood chips to the side tray

Take a small-sized bowl and add brown sugar, paprika, chipotle, mustard, salt and cumin

Transfer the chicken wings to a large resealable bag and pour the seasoning mix

Seal and shake the chicken

Refrigerate for 60 minutes

Preheat your Smoker to 250 degrees Fahrenheit with oak woods

Transfer the chicken to your smoker rack and Smoke for 1 and a ½ to 2 hours

Check if the internal temperature is 165 degrees Fahrenheit and serve!

Nutrition Values (Per Serving)

Calories: 180

Fats: 7g

Carbs: 3g

Fiber: 1g

Herby Quail

Serving: 3

Prep Time: 10 minutes

Cook Time: 1 hour

Recommended Wood Type: Hickory Wood

Ingredients

- 4-6 quail
- 2 tablespoon of olive oil
- Salt as needed
- Freshly ground black pepper
- 1 pack of dry Hidden Valley Ranch dressing (or your preferred one)
- ½ a cup of melted butter

How To

Take your drip pan and add water, cover with aluminum foil. Pre-heat your smoker to 225 degrees F

Use water fill water pan halfway through and place it over drip pan. Add wood chips to the side tray

Brush the quail with olive oil and season with salt and pepper

Place the in your smoker and smoke for 1 hour

Take a small bowl and add ranch dressing mix and melted butter

After the first 30 minutes of smoking, brush the quail with the ranch mix

Repeat at the end of the cooking time

Once the internal temperature of the quail reaches 145 degrees Fahrenheit, they are ready!

Nutrition Values (Per Serving)

Calories: 209

Fats: 13g

Carbs: 0g

Fiber: 3g

Tequila Lime Roasted Turkey

Prep Time: 25 Minutes

Cooking Time: 2 Hours & 35 Minutes

Servings: 12 Persons

Ingredients

- 9 garlic cloves
- 1 bone-in whole turkey (roughly 15 pounds), thawed
- 3 jalapeño chiles, cut in half & seeded
- 1 ¼ cups gold tequila
- 3 ounces' olive oil
- 1 ½ teaspoons pepper
- 3 limes, cut into wedges
- 1 ¼ cups lime juice, fresh
- ¾ cups each of orange juice & chicken broth
- 3 tablespoon chili powder
- 1 tablespoon salt

Directions

Preheat your smoker to 325 F in advance. Place the turkey breast in a shallow roasting pan, preferably pores and skin aspect up.

Place the jalapeno & garlic in a mini meals processor. Cover & process on high strength until chopped finely. Add the chili powder observed by using three oz. of tequila, three oz. of lime juice, oil, pepper and salt. Cover & method on high electricity again till the aggregate is completely smooth.

Next, the usage of spoon or fingers; loosen the turkey pores and skin & rub the organized garlic aggregate over and underneath the turkey pores and skin; calmly pour the leftover blend on top of the turkey. Insert an ovenproof meat thermometer into the thickest part of the breast & make certain that it doesn't' t touch the bone.

Pour the broth and orange juice observed by using the leftover lime juice and tequila into a roasting pan.

Roast until the thermometer displays an analyzing of one hundred 65 F, uncovered.

Place the turkey on a warm platter and then, cover with aluminum foil. Let stand for 12 to 15 minutes before carving. Spoon the pan juices on pinnacle of the turkey & garnish your dish with some clean lime wedges. Enjoy.

Nutritional Value

517 Calories, 341 Calories from Fat

38g Total Fat, 17g Saturated Fat

1.8g Polyunsaturated Fat, 18g Monounsaturated Fat

154mg Cholesterol, 118mg Sodium

558mg Potassium, 0.3g Total Carbohydrates, 0g Dietary Fiber

0g Sugars, 44g Protein

Smoked Chicken Legs

Serving: 4

Prep Time: 20 minutes

Cook Time: 90 minutes

Recommended Wood Type: Hickory

Ingredients

- ½ cup parmesan cheese
- 3 tablespoons garlic powder
- ½ cup butter, melted
- ½ cup chicken wing rub, your choice
- 6 chicken legs

How To

Take your drip pan and add water, cover with aluminum foil. Pre-heat your smoker to 275 degrees F

Use water fill water pan halfway through and place it over drip pan. Add wood chips to the side tray

Season chicken legs with wing rub, mix in butter and garlic well

Add chicken to the smoker, keep smoking for 90 minutes until the internal temperature is 165 degrees F, making sure to flip it after every 30 minutes

Remove and transfer to Iron Skillet

Sprinkle parmesan cheese and cook for 10-15 minutes more until the cheese melts completely

Enjoy!

Nutrition Values (Per Serving)

Calories: 932

Fat: 66g

Carbohydrates: 24g

Protein: 62g

Grilled Chicken with Banana Peppers

Ingredients

- 2 finely grated garlic cloves
- 2 tbsp. of fresh lime juice 1 tbsp. fish sauce
- 1 tbsp. of cayenne pepper
- 1 tbsp. dark brown sugar
- 1 tbsp. garlic powder
- 2 tsp crushed red pepper flakes
- 2 tsp dried thyme
- 2 tsp ground allspice
- 2 tsp of onion powder
- 1 tsp grounded black pepper
- 1 tsp paprika
- ½ tsp ground cinnamon
- ½ tsp. of ground nutmeg
- 3 tbsp. vegetable oil and more for the grill
- 16 skin on, bone-in, chicken thighs (about 5½ lb.) Kosher salt
- 16 banana pepper thinly sliced lime wedges and chopped cilantro

Recipe Preparation

Put the garlic, lime juice, fish sauce, the cayenne, sugar, the garlic powder, purple pepper flakes, the dried thyme, the grounded allspice, onion powder, black pepper, the paprika, cinnamon, nutmeg and 3 tbsp. of oil in a huge bowl. Add the chook and season with salt. Let it sit down, turning chicken thighs once, for at the least two hours or kick back for one day.

Set up the grill for medium-high and indirect warmness and oil the grate. Put the chicken thighs, pores and skin side down, on the grate over the hottest a part of the grill and grill them, turning as soon as, till lightly burned, approximately 5 to 10 minutes. Move the fowl onto the cooler a part of the grill and preserve grilling, turning many times, till the instant-study thermometer inserted into the thickest element registers 165°, greater or less 20–25 minutes longer. Place the fowl onto a platter and allow it rest for ten minutes.

Top it with the banana peppers and cilantro and serve with lime wedges.

Smoked Up Chicken Wrap

Serving: 4

Prep Time: 10-15 minutes

Cook Time: 3 hours

Recommended Wood Type: Maple Wood

Ingredients

- 2 small chicken breasts
- Romaine's hearts
- 1 tomato, diced
- Shavings of parmesan cheese
- Caesar salad dressing
- 1 teaspoon salt
- 1 teaspoon pepper
- ½ teaspoon garlic powder
- 4 large tortillas

How To

Take your drip pan and add water, cover with aluminum foil. Preheat your Smoker to 225 degrees F

Take a large bowl and add breasts, season with salt and pepper, garlic powder

Use water fill water pan halfway through and place it over drip pan. Add wood chips to the side tray.

Transfer chicken to Smoker and Smoke for 1 and ½ hours until internal temperature reaches 165 degrees F

Remove chicken once done, let it rest for 10 minutes, cut into slices

Take a large mixing bowl and add romaine hearts, Caesar dressing, parmesan cheese shavings

Mix well

Warm tortillas on a flat pan on the stove and transfer toasted tortilla to a tray

Put a layer of salad, tomatoes, chicken slices and spoonful of dressing on top

Fold into rolls and enjoy!

Nutrition Values (Per Serving)

Calories: 530

Fat: 23g

Carbohydrates: 52g

Protein: 31g

Smoked Butter Chicken

Serving: 8

Prep Time: 30 minutes

Cook Time: 1 and ½ hours

Recommended Wood Type: Apple/Olive Chips

Ingredients

- 2 pound of skinless chicken breast, cut up into 1-inch pieces
- 5 tablespoons of divided butter
- 1 cup of sour cream
- 1 tablespoon of freshly squeezed lemon juice
- 2 tablespoon of divided chili powder
- 2 and a ½ tablespoon of Garam Masala
- 2 tablespoon + 2 extra teaspoons of garlic, minced
- 2 teaspoon of coarse kosher salt
- 1 jalapeno chile, seeded and minced
- 1 tablespoon of sugar
- 1 teaspoon of ground coriander
- 1 can tomatoes, crushed
- 1 tablespoon of tomato paste
- ¾ cup of heavy cream
- Cooked rice or Naan Bread

How To

Take a 1-gallon zip bag and toss in your chicken breast

Melt about 3 tablespoons of butter and toss it in your bag alongside the lemon juice, sour cream, 1 tablespoon of chili powder, 1 tablespoon of Garam masala, 2 teaspoons of ginger, 2 teaspoons of garlic and 1 teaspoon of salt

Seal up your bag and massage it nicely

Then marinate for about 3 hours

Take your drip pan and add water, cover with aluminum foil. Pre-heat your smoker to 275 degrees F

Use water fill water pan halfway through and place it over drip pan. Add wood chips to the side tray

Pour in your chicken marinade into a 10 inch sized iron skillet and place it on top of your smoker

Cook for 30 minutes without adding the chips

While the chicken is being cooked, add in the 2 tablespoons of butter, 2 tablespoons of garlic to the skillet alongside the jalapeno and onions

Place another skillet n your stovetop over medium-high heat for about 3-5 minutes

Stir in the sugar, coriander, 1 tablespoon of chili powder and 1 and a ½ tablespoon of Garam masala to make the sauce

Cook for 1 minute and once you can feel the fragrance, toss in the crushed tomatoes

Keep stirring occasionally

Remove the heat from your skillet and remove the skillet from your smoker

Pour in the sauce into the skillet with the chicken and stir nicely to combines

Return the skillet with chicken back to the smoker

Close up the door of your smoker and toss in the soaked pecan chips now

Add in more chips and sauce after 30 minutes of cooking

The chicken will be done once the internal temperature comes at 165 degrees Fahrenheit which should take around 1 hour

Remove the skillet and serve with either rice or bread

Nutrition Values (Per Serving)

Calories: 362

Fats: 67g

Carbs: 56g

Fiber: 15g

Plum Chicken Pop

Serving: 3

Prep Time: 35 minutes

Cook Time: 2 hours

Recommended Wood Type: Cherry Wood

Ingredients

- 12 chicken drumsticks
- 2 teaspoons of salt
- 2 teaspoon of fresh ground black pepper
- Plum sauce (homemade or store-bought)

How To

Take your drip pan and add water, cover with aluminum foil. Preheat your Smoker to 225 degrees F

Use water fill water pan halfway through and place it over drip pan. Add wood chips to the side tray

Stretch the skin away from drumsticks as much as possible

Remove the tendons from each leg

Season the drumsticks with salt and pepper and transfer to your smoker rack

Smoker for 1 and a ½ hours

Baste the pops with plum sauce and transfer to Smoker again, a smoker for 30 minutes until the internal temperature reaches 165 degrees Fahrenheit

Allow them to rest for a while

Coat the meat with more sauce and enjoy!

Nutrition Values (Per Serving)

Calories: 222

Fats: 11g

Carbs: 16g

Fiber: 3g

Chesapeake Garlic Parmesan Wings

Prep Time: 15 Minutes

Cooking Time: 1 Hour & 35 Minutes

Servings: 6 Persons

Ingredients

- For Wings
- 2 to 4 pounds' chicken wings
- Pepper & salt to taste
- For Garlic Parmesan Sauce
- 1 cup hot sauce, any of your favorite
- 2 tablespoons parmesan, grated
- 1 stick of butter
- 2 tablespoons minced garlic
- 1 teaspoon old bay seasoning
- ¼ cup raw honey

Directions

Preheat your pellet grill at 350 F earlier.

Cook the bird wings till an inner temperature displays one hundred 45 F.

In the meantime, put together the sauce. Next, over mild warmness in a big sauce pan; warmness the complete sauce substances collectively.

Slowly upload the butter & deliver the elements a great stir until the butter is melted completely. Continue to stir the ingredient till the sauce elements and butter are mixed calmly; set the aggregate aside.

Prepare a Dutch oven with oil for frying. Heat the oil until very hot.

five. Remove the hen pieces from smoker & positioned the hen into the fry basket. Fry the bird for more than one minutes, till they reflect internal temperature of a hundred sixty-five F.

Place the cooked wings on a baking sheet lined with paper towel & maintain to cook for 5 to 10 extra mins.

Toss the wings with organized sauce till protected completely.

Serve hot and enjoy.

Nutritional Value

1035 Calories

712 Calories from Fat

79g Total Fat, 35g Saturated Fat

1.5g Trans Fat, 11g Polyunsaturated Fat

27g Monounsaturated Fat

249mg Cholesterol, 2785mg Sodium

513mg Potassium

43g Total Carbohydrates

1.3g Dietary Fiber

19g Sugars, 40g Protein

Alderwood Turkey Breast

Serving: 4

Prep Time: 20 minutes + marinating time

Cook Time: 3 and ¼ hours

Recommended Wood Type: Apple Wood

Ingredients

- 4 tablespoon of unsalted butter
- 8 teaspoon of Dijon mustard
- 2 tablespoons of chopped fresh thyme leaves
- 1 teaspoon of freshly ground black pepper
- ½ a teaspoon of kosher salt
- 1 bone-in turkey breast

How To

Take a small-sized bowl and stir in butter, thyme, mustard, ¼ teaspoon of pepper, salt

Rub the turkey breast with the butter mix

Cover and allow it to refrigerate overnight

Take your drip pan and add water, cover with aluminum foil. Preheat your Smoker to 225 degrees F

Use water fill water pan halfway through and place it over drip pan. Add wood chips to the side tray

Sprinkle breast with ¾ teaspoon of pepper and transfer to smoker rack

Cover and smoke for 3 and a ½ to 4 hours, making sure to keep adding more chips after every 60 minutes

Once the internal temperature reaches 165 degrees Fahrenheit, remove the turkey and allow it to rest

Slice and serve!

Nutrition Values (Per Serving)

Calories: 238

Fats: 11g

Carbs: 40g

Fiber: 1g

Sizzling' Buffalo Wings

Preparation time: 10 minutes

Cooking time: 40 minutes

Servings: 8

Ingredients:

- 36 chicken wings, separated
- 1 tbsp. vegetable oil
- 1 tsp. salt
- 1 cup all-purpose flour
- 1 ½ tbsp. white vinegar
- 1/4 tsp. cayenne pepper
- 1/4 tsp. garlic powder
- 1 tsp. Tabasco sauce
- 1/4 tsp. Worcestershire sauce
- 1/4 tsp. seasoned salt
- 6 tbsp. Frank's Red-Hot Sauce
- 6 tbsp. unsalted butter
- Celery sticks blue cheese dressing
- Intolerances:
- Gluten-Free
- Egg-Free

Directions:

Mix all except chicken, salt, oil and flour in a pan, bring to a simmer, stirring, and then cool.

Toss the wings with the oil, and salt. Place into a large plastic bag, add the flour, and shake to coat evenly. Remove from the bag, shaking off excess flour.

Place wings on hot pellet grill, turning several times until golden brown.

Remove wings from grill and place them in a sealed bowl with the sauce and shake well.

Serve immediately with blue cheese and chilled celery sticks.

Nutrition:

Calories: 130

Fat: 6g

Carbs: 6g

Protein: 10g

Sriracha BBQ Chicken

Serving: 5

Prep Time: 30 minutes

Cook Time: 1-2 hours

Recommended Wood Type: Cherry Wood

Ingredients

- 1 cup of sriracha
- ½ a cup of butter
- ½ a cup of molasses
- ½ a cup of ketchup
- ¼ cup of firmly packed brown sugar
- ¼ cup of prepared yellow mustard
- 1 teaspoon of salt
- 1 teaspoon of freshly ground black pepper
- 1 whole chicken, cut into pieces
- ½ a teaspoon of freshly chopped parsley leaves

How To

Take your drip pan and add water, cover with aluminum foil. Preheat your Smoker to 250 degrees F

Use water fill water pan halfway through and place it over drip pan. Add wood chips to the side tray

Take a medium saucepan and place it over low heat, stir in butter, sriracha, ketchup, molasses, brown sugar, mustard, pepper and salt and keep stirring until the sugar and salt dissolves

Divide the sauce into two portions

Brush the chicken half with the sauce and reserve the remaining for serving

Make sure to keep the sauce for serving on the side, and keep the other portion for basting

Transfer chicken to your smoker rack and smoke for about 1 and a ½ to 2 hours until the internal temperature reaches 165 degrees Fahrenheit

Sprinkle chicken with parsley and serve with reserved BBQ sauce

Enjoy!

Nutrition Values (Per Serving)

Calories: 148

Fats: 0.6g

Carbs: 10g

Fiber: 1g

Mesquite Bacon And Maple Chicken

Serving: 7

Prep Time: 20 minutes

Cook Time: 1 and 1/2 hours

Recommended Wood Type: Cherry Wood

Ingredients

- 4 boneless and skinless chicken breasts
- Salt as needed
- Freshly ground black pepper
- 12 slices of uncooked bacon
- 1 cup of maple syrup
- ½ a cup of melted butter
- 1 teaspoon of liquid smoke

How To

Take your drip pan and add water, cover with aluminum foil. Pre-heat your smoker to 225 degrees F

Use water fill water pan halfway through and place it over drip pan. Add wood chips to the side tray

Season the chicken with pepper and salt

Wrap the breast with 3 bacon slices and cover the entire surface

Secure the bacon with toothpicks

Take a medium-sized bowl and stir in maple syrup, butter, liquid smoker and mix well

Reserve 1/3 rd of this mixture for later use

Submerge the chicken breast into the butter mix and coat them well

Place a pan in your smoker and transfer the chicken to your smoker

Smoker for 1 to 1 and a ½ hours

Brush the chicken with reserved butter and smoke for 30 minutes more until the internal temperature reaches 165-degree Fahrenheit

Enjoy!

Nutrition Values (Per Serving)

Calories: 458

Fats: 20g

Carbs: 65g

Fiber: 1g

Grilled Chicken Drumsticks with Savory Caramel

Ingredients

- Vegetable oil (for the grill)
- 4 grated garlic cloves
- 1 grated lemongrass stalk
- ½ cup sugar
- ¼ cup unseasoned rice vinegar
- 2 tsp crushed red pepper flakes
- 2 tsp grounded cumin
- 1 tsp grounded black pepper
- 3 tbsp. fish sauce
- 12 large chicken drumsticks (about 3 lb.)
- Kosher salt

Recipe Preparation

Set up the grill for pinnacle indirect heat. Add the garlic, lemongrass, sugar, the vinegar, crimson pepper flakes, cumin, the black pepper, and ½ cup water to boil in a small pan, stirring occasionally and cook until reduced to ½ cup, about eight minutes. Let it cool and add inside the fish sauce. Move half of the sauce to a tiny bowl and positioned aside for serving.

Season the chicken with salt. Put the hen over oblique warmness. Grill, turning once or twice, till the pores and skin is singed and crisp and meat is cooked through, approximately 25–30 minutes. Move the hen to the hotter part of the grill and maintain grilling, turning frequently and spooning with the final sauce, until covered and lightly burned in places, 6 to 8 minutes longer. Serve with reserved sauce.

Bacon Cordon Bleu

Preparation time: 30 minutes

Cooking time: 2 hours

Servings: 6

Ingredients:

- 24 bacon slices
- 3 large boneless, skinless chicken breasts, butterfly
- 3 extra virgin olive oils with roasted garlic flavor
- 3 Yang original dry lab or poultry seasonings
- 12 slice black forest ham
- 12-slice provolone cheese
- Intolerances:
- Gluten-Free
- Egg-Free

Directions:

Weave 4 slices of bacon tightly, leaving extra space on the edges. Bacon weave is used to interlock alternating bacon slices and wrap chicken cordon blue.

Slice or rub two chicken breast fillets with olive oil on both sides.

Sprinkle the seasoning on both sides of the chicken breast.

Lay the seasoned chicken fillets on the bacon weave and slice one ham and one provolone cheese on each.

Repeat this process with another chicken fillet, ham and cheese. Fold chicken, ham and cheese in half.

Lay the bacon strips from the opposite corner to completely cover the chicken cordon blue.

Use a silicon food grade cooking band, butcher twine, and toothpick to secure the bacon strip in place.

Repeat this process for the remaining chicken breast and ingredients.

Using apple or cherry pellets, configure a wood pellet smoker grill for indirect cooking and preheat (180°F to 200°F) for smoking. Inhale bacon cordon blue for 1 hour.

After smoking for 1 hour, raise the pit temperature to 350°F.

Bacon cordon blue occurs when the internal temperature reaches 165°F and the bacon becomes crispy.

Rest for 15 minutes under a loose foil tent before serving.

Nutrition:

Calories: 230

Fat: 2g

Cholesterol: 78mg

Carbs: 13g

Protein: 38g

Duck Poppers

Preparation time: 15 minutes

Cooking time: 30 minutes

Servings: 1

Ingredients:

- 8 – 10 pieces of bacon, cut event into same-sized pieces measuring 4 inches each
- 3 duck breasts; boneless and with skin removed and sliced into strips measuring ½ inches
- Sriracha sauce
- 6 de-seeded jalapenos, with the top cut off and sliced into strips
- Intolerances:
- Gluten-Free
- Egg-Free
- Lactose-Free

Directions:

Wrap the bacon around one trip of pepper and one slice of duck.

Secure it firmly with the help of a toothpick.

Fire the grill on low flame and keep this wrap and grill it for half an hour until the bacon turns crisp.

Rotate often to ensure even cooking.

Serve with sriracha sauce.

Nutrition:

Calories: 337 Fat: 30g Cholesterol: 143mg Carbs: 19g Protein: 12g

Spiced Lemon Chicken

Preparation time: 20 minutes

Cooking time: 1 hour and 10 minutes

Servings: 1

Ingredients:

- 1 whole chicken
- 4 cloves of minced garlic
- Zest of 2 fresh lemons
- 1 tbsp of olive oil
- 1 tbsp of smoked paprika
- 1 ½ tsp of salt
- ½ tsp of black pepper
- ½ tsp of dried oregano
- 1 tbsp of ground cumin
- Intolerances:
- Gluten-Free
- Egg-Free
- Lactose-Free

Directions:

Preheat the grill by pushing the temperature to 375°F.

Take the chicken and spatchcock it by cutting it on both sides right from the backbone to the tail via the neck.

Lay it flat and push it down on the breastbone. This would break the ribs.

Take all the leftover ingredients in a bowl except ½ tsp of salt and crush them to make a smooth rub.

Spread this rub evenly over the chicken, making sure that it seeps right under the skin.

Place the chicken on the grill grates and cook for an hour until the internal temperature reads 165°F. Let it rest for 10 minutes.

Serve and enjoy.

Nutrition:

Calories: 178

Fat: 9g

Protein: 23g

Citrus Packed Chicken Meal

Serving: 3

Prep Time: 15 minutes

Cook Time: 18 hours 5 minutes

Recommended Wood Type: Peach/Maple Wood

Ingredients

- 1 whole chicken, pieced
- 4 cups of lemon-lime flavored carbonated beverage
- 1 tablespoon of garlic powder
- 2 cups of soaked wood chips

How To

Transfer the whole chicken to a large-sized zip bag

Sprinkle garlic powder and pour lemon-lime soda mix into the bag

Seal the bag and allow it to marinate overnight

Take your drip pan and add water, cover with aluminum foil. Pre-heat your smoker to 225 degrees F

Use water fill water pan halfway through and place it over drip pan. Add wood chips to the side tray

Remove the chicken from the bag and transfer to your smoker rack

Discard the marinade

Smoker for 10 hours, making sure keep adding more wood chips after every hour

Serve and enjoy!

Nutrition Values (Per Serving)

Calories: 644

Fats: 34g

Carbs: 19g

Fiber: 0.1g

Smoked Rosemary Chicken Kebab

Serving: 4

Prep Time: 10 + minutes

Cook Time: 1 and ½ hours

Recommended Wood Type: Hickory

Ingredients

- 5 boneless, skinless chicken breasts, cubed
- The Rub
- ½ cup ranch dressing
- ½ cup olive oil
- 1 tablespoon fresh rosemary, minced
- 3 tablespoons Worcestershire sauce
- 1 teaspoon lemon juice
- 2 teaspoons salt
- ¼ teaspoon pepper
- 1 teaspoon white vinegar
- 1 tablespoon sugar

How To

Prepare marinade by adding ranch dressing, olive oil, rosemary, sauce, lemon juice, salt, vinegar, sugar in a bowl and mix well

Let it stand for a while

Add chicken and toss well, let it chill for 30 minutes

Thread cubes onto skewers and arrange on a lightly oiled grid

Take your drip pan and add water, cover with aluminum foil. Pre-heat your smoker to 275 degrees F

Use water fill water pan halfway through and place it over drip pan. Add wood chips to the side tray

Smoke for 90 minutes until cook well

Enjoy!

Nutrition Values (Per Serving)

Calories: 408

Fat: 20g

Carbohydrates: 18g

Protein: 38g

Turkey Parmigiana

Serving: 4

Prep Time: 20 minutes

Cook Time: 2 hours

Recommended Wood Type: Hickory

Ingredients

- 1 pound turkey breast fillets, boneless
- The Rub
- 2 egg whites
- 1 tablespoon water
- 2 tablespoons seasoned Italian breadcrumbs
- 2 tablespoons parmesan cheese
- 1 cup marinara sauce
- 1 cup mozzarella sauce, shredded

How To

Whisk in egg whites and water in a shallow dish, take another dish and add breadcrumbs and parmesan

Dip each turkey fillet first in egg whites and then in bread crumbs

Arrange the meat in pan and place on cooking

Take your drip pan and add water, cover with aluminum foil. Pre-heat your smoker to 275 degrees F

Use water fill water pan halfway through and place it over drip pan. Add wood chips to the side tray

Smoke for 120 minutes, pour marinara sauce over breaded turkey and sprinkle over mozzarella

Cook for 5 minutes more until cheese melts

Enjoy!

Nutrition Values (Per Serving)

Calories: 408

Fat: 20g

Carbohydrates: 18g

Protein: 38g

Roast Duck a L'Orange

Preparation time: 30 minutes

Cooking time: 2 to 2.5 hours

Serve: 4

Ingredients:

- 1 (5-6 lb.) Frozen Long Island, Beijing or Canadian ducks
- 3 tbsp west or 3 tbsp
- 1 large orange, cut into wedges
- 3 celery stems chopped into large chunks
- 1/2 small red onion, a quarter
- Orange Sauce:
- 2 orange cups
- 2 tablespoons soy sauce
- 2 tablespoons orange marmalade
- 2 tablespoons honey
- 3g tsp grated raw
- Intolerances:
- Gluten-Free
- Egg-Free
- Lactose-Free

Directions:

Remove the nibble from the duck's cavity and neck. Rinse the duck and pat dry with a paper towel.

Remove excess fat from tail, neck and cavity. Use a sharp scalpel knife tip to pierce the duck's skin entirely, so that it does not penetrate the duck's meat, to help dissolve the fat layer beneath the skin.

Add the seasoning inside the cavity with one cup of rub or seasoning.

Season the outside of the duck with the remaining friction or seasoning.

Fill the cavity with orange wedges, celery and onion. Duck legs are tied with butcher twine to make filling easier. Place the duck breast up on a small rack of shallow roast bread.

To make the sauce, mix the ingredients in the saucepan over low heat and cook until the sauce is thick and syrupy. Set aside and let cool.

Set the wood pellet smoker grill for indirect cooking and use the pellets to preheat to 350°F.

Roast the ducks at 350°F for 2 hours.

After 2 hours, brush the duck freely with orange sauce.

Roast the orange glass duck for another 30 minutes, making sure that the inside temperature of the thickest part of the leg reaches 165°F.

Place duck under loose foil tent for 20 minutes before serving.

Serve.

Nutrition:

Calories: 467, Fat: 24g, Cholesterol: 221mg, Carbs: 6g, Protein: 51g

Lemon Cornish Chicken Stuffed with Crab Meat

Preparation time: 30 minutes

Cooking time: 1 hour 30 minutes

Serve: 2 – 4

Ingredients:

- 2 Cornish chickens (about 1¾ pound each)
- Half lemon, half
- 4 tbsp western rub or poultry rub
- 2 cups stuffed with crab meat
- Intolerances:
- Gluten-Free
- Egg-Free
- Lactose-Free

Directions:

Rinse chicken thoroughly inside and outside, tap lightly and let it dry.

Carefully loosen the skin on the chest and legs. Rub the lemon under and over the skin and into the cavity. Rub the western lab under and over the skin on the chest and legs. Carefully return the skin to its original position.

Wrap the Cornish hen in plastic wrap and refrigerate for 2-3 hours until flavor is absorbed.

Prepare crab meat stuffing. Make sure it is completely cooled before packing the chicken. Loosely fill the cavities of each hen with crab filling.

Tie the Cornish chicken legs with a butcher's leash to put the filling.

Set wood pellet smoker grill for indirect cooking and preheat to 375°F with pellets.

Place the stuffed animal on the rack in the baking dish. If you do not have a rack that is small enough to fit, you can also place the chicken directly on the baking dish.

Roast the chicken at 375°F until the inside temperature of the thickest part of the chicken breast reaches 170°F, the thigh reaches 180°F, and the juice is clear.

Test the crab meat stuffing to see if the temperature has reached 165°F.

Place the roasted chicken under a loose foil tent for 15 minutes before serving.

Nutrition:

Calories: 660

Fat: 47g

Protein: 57g

Roasted Tuscan Thighs

Preparation time: 20 minutes

Cooking time: 40 minutes – 1 hour

Servings: 4

Ingredients:

- 8 chicken thighs, with bone, with skin
- 3 extra virgin olive oils with roasted garlic flavor
- 3 cups of Tuscan or Tuscan seasoning per thigh
- Intolerances:
- Gluten-Free
- Egg-Free
- Lactose-Free

Directions:

Cut off excess skin on chicken thighs and leave at 1/4 inch to shrink.

Carefully peel off the skin and remove large deposits of fat under the skin and behind the thighs.

Lightly rub olive oil behind and below the skin and thighs. A seasoning from Tuscan, seasoned on the skin of the thigh and the top and bottom of the back.

Wrap chicken thighs in plastic wrap, refrigerate for 1-2 hours, allow time for flavor to be absorbed before roasting.

Set the wood pellet smoker grill for indirect cooking and use the pellets to preheat to 375°F.

Roast for 40-60 minutes until the internal temperature of the thick part of the chicken thigh reaches 180°F.

Place the roasted Tuscan thighs under a loose foil tent for 15 minutes before serving.

Nutrition:

Calories: 177

Fat: 8g

Cholesterol: 135mg

Protein: 25g

Smoked Turkey

Prep Time: 20 Minutes

Cooking Time: 1 Hour & 55 Minutes

Servings: 10 Persons

Ingredients

- 1 whole turkey
- ½ lemon, medium-sized
- Poultry rub, any of your favorite to coat
- 1 stick of softened butter, at room temperature
- ½ cup of white wine, chicken broth or liquid of choice
- 2 tablespoons each of pepper & salt

Directions

Preheat your pellet grill over high smoke in advance.

Remove the neck and giblets from the turkey then, rinse under water; pat it dry the use of paper towels.

Next, combine the butter with pepper and salt in a small-sized mixing bowl.

Gently separate the pores and skin from legs and breast using your hands (make certain that you hold it attached & in a single piece).

Pour & evenly spread the prepared butter combination under the skin. Season the turkey with the poultry seasoning (at the outer part).

Fill the Turkey Cannon Infusion Roaster with approximately lemon & ½ cup of liquid. Next, smoke the turkey on high smoke for an hour. Set the temperature of your pellet grill to 350 F & continue to prepare dinner the turkey until the internal temperature of the meat displays a hundred and sixty F. Set aside & let relaxation more or less for 1/2 an hour.

Serve and enjoy.

Nutritional Value

873 Calories

359 Calories from Fat

40g Total Fat

14g Saturated Fat

0.7g Trans Fat

8.3g Polyunsaturated Fat

12g Monounsaturated Fat

416mg Cholesterol 1990mg Sodium

1253mg Potassium

2.2g Total Carbohydrates

0.4g Dietary Fiber

0.6g Sugars 50g Protein

Baked Garlic Parmesan Wings

Preparation time: 20 minutes

Cooking time: 30 minutes

Servings: 1

Ingredients:

- 5 lbs. of chicken wings
- ½ cup of chicken rub
- For the garnish:
- 1 cup of shredded parmesan cheese
- 3 tbsp of chopped parsley
- For the Sauce:
- 10 cloves of finely diced garlic
- 1 cup of butter
- 2 tbsp of chicken rub
- Intolerances:
- Gluten-Free
- Egg-Free

Directions:

Set the grill on preheat by keeping the temperature high.

Take a large bowl and toss the wings in it along with the chicken rub.

Place the wings directly on the grill grate and cook it for 10 minutes.

Flip it and cook for the next ten minutes.

Check the internal temperature, and it needs to reach in the range of 165 to 180°F.

For the garlic Sauce:

Take a midsized saucepan and mix garlic, butter, and the leftover rub.

Cook it over medium heat on a stovetop for 10 minutes while stirring in between to avoid the making of lumps.

When the wings have been cooked, remove them from the grill and place in a large bowl.

Toss the wings with garlic sauce along with parsley and parmesan cheese.

Serve and enjoy.

Nutrition:

Calories: 90

Fat: 8g

Cholesterol: 22mg

Carbs: 1g

Protein: 4g

Cajun Patch Cock Chicken

Preparation time: 30 minutes

Cooking time: 2 hours and 30 minutes

Servings: 4

Ingredients:

- 4-5 pounds of fresh or thawed frozen chicken
- 4-6 glasses of extra virgin olive oil
- Cajun Spice 4 tablespoons or Lucile Bloody Mary Mix Cajun Hot Dry Herb Mix Seasoning
- Intolerances:
- Gluten-Free
- Egg-Free
- Lactose-Free

Directions:

Place the chicken breast on a cutting board with the chest down.

Using kitchen or poultry scissors, cut along the side of the spine and remove.

Turn the chicken over and press down firmly on the chest to flatten it. Carefully loosen and remove the skin on the chest, thighs and drumsticks.

Rub olive oil freely under and on the skin. Season chicken in all directions and apply directly to the meat under the skin.

Wrap the chicken in plastic wrap and place in the refrigerator for 3 hours to absorb the flavor.

Use hickory, pecan pellets, or blend to configure a wood pellet smoker grill for indirect cooking and preheat to 225°F.

If the unit has a temperature meat probe input, such as a MAK Grills 2 Star, insert the probe into the thickest part of the breast. Make chicken for 1 1/2 hours.

After one and a half hours at 225°F, raise the pit temperature to 375°F and roast until the inside temperature of the thickest part of the chest reaches 170°F and the thighs are at least 180°F.

Place the chicken under a loose foil tent for 15 minutes before carving.

Nutrition:

Calories: 308

Fat: 18g

Carbs: 1g

Protein: 30g

Flattened Mojo Chicken

Preparation time: 25 minutes

Cooking time: 1 hour

Servings: 12

Ingredients:

- 3 – 4 lb. whole chickens
- 3 tbsp. olive oil
- 6 cups Traditional Cuban Mojo
- 3 tsp. sea salt
- 3 tbsp. Adobo Criollo spices
- Intolerances:
- Gluten-Free
- Egg-Free
- Lactose-Free

Directions:

Rinse chicken with cold water and pat dry. Cut out backbone with kitchen shears.

Turn chicken breast side up and open like a book. Press down firmly on breast to flatten and break rib bones. Loosen skin from body under breast and thighs.

Place each chicken in a gallon-size resealable bag with 2 cups Mojo.

Marinate (flat) in refrigerator 24 hours. Remove chickens from bags and discard mojo.

Blot each bird dry, and rub each with 1 Tbsp. olive oil, and then 1 Tbsp. Adobo Criollo spice blend.

Pre-heat one side of your pellet grill; and leave one side unlighted, cover and preheat for 20 minutes.

Place chicken skin side down in the middle of the grill with legs closest to the heat.

Watch carefully and turn over when skin starts to brown. Turn and move chicken to the "cool" side and cover with a large disposable aluminum pan (a favorite restaurant trick.)

Cooking time will vary, depending on the fire and the size of the chicken.

Check the temperature at 20 minutes after turning. When the temperature in the thigh reaches 175 degrees, remove from the heat and let sit, loosely covered for 15 minutes.

Nutrition:

Calories: 160

Fat: 10g

Carbs: 1g

Protein: 20g

Peanut Chicken Satay

Preparation time: 20 minutes

Cooking time: 40 minutes

Servings: 8

Ingredients:

- 4 tbsp. olive oil
- 4 tbsp. sesame oil
- 2 tsp. ginger powder
- 2 tsp. powdered garlic
- 2 tbsp. curry powder Butter lettuce leaves
- 20 wooden skewers, soaked Fresh cilantro leaves
- 2 lbs. chicken thighs, cut into strips
- Peanut Sauce:
- 2 cups chunky peanut butter
- 1/2 cups soy sauce
- 1/4 cup brown sugar
- 1/4 cup sweet chili paste
- 1/3 cup limes juice
- 2/3 cup hot water
- Intolerances:

- Gluten-Free
- Egg-Free

Directions:

Combine oils, ginger, garlic, and curry powder in a shallow mixing bowl. Place the chicken strips in the marinade and gently toss until well coated.

Cover and let the chicken marinate in the refrigerator overnight.

Thread the chicken pieces onto the soaked skewers working the skewer in and out of the meat, down the middle of the piece, so that it stays in place during grilling.

Brush pellet grill with oil to prevent the meat from sticking. Grill the satays for 3 to 5 minutes on each side, until nicely seared and cooked through.

Serve on a platter lined with lettuce leaves and cilantro; accompanied by a small bowl of peanut sauce on the side.

For the Sauce:

Combine the peanut butter, soy sauce, chili paste, brown sugar, and lime juice in a food processor or blender. Puree to combine, and drizzle in the hot water to thin out the sauce.

Pour the sauce into individual serving bowls.

Nutrition:

Calories: 185, Fat: 9g, Carbs: 5g, Protein: 20g

PORK RECIPES

Grilled Carnitas

Preparation time: 20 minutes

Cook time: 10 hours

Servings: 12

Ingredients:

- 1 tsp paprika
- 1 tsp oregano
- 1 tsp cayenne pepper
- 2 tsp brown sugar
- 1 tsp mint
- 1 tbsp onion powder
- 1 tsp cumin
- 1 tsp chili powder
- 2 tbsp salt
- 1 tsp garlic powder
- 1 tsp Italian seasoning

- 2 tbsp olive oil.

- 5 pounds pork shoulder roast

- Intolerances:

- Gluten-Free

- Egg-Free

- Lactose-Free

Directions:

Trim the pork of any excess fat.

To make rub, combine the paprika, oregano, cayenne, sugar, mint, onion powder, garlic powder, cumin, chili, salt, and Italian seasoning in a small mixing bowl.

Rub all sides of the pork with the rub.

Start your grill for smoking, leaving the lid open until fire starts.

Close the lid and preheat grill to 325°F with lid closed for 15 minutes.

Place the pork in a foil pan and place the pan on the grill—Cook for about 2 hours.

After 2 hours, increase the heat to 325°F and smoke pork for an additional 8 hours or until the pork's internal temperature reaches 190°F.

Remove pork from it and let it sit until it is cook and easy to handle.

Shred the pork with two forks.

Place a cast-iron skillet on the grill grate and add the olive oil.

Add the pork and sear until the pork is brown and crispy.

Remove pork from heat and let it rest for a few minutes.

Serve.

Nutrition:

Calories: 514

Fat: 41.1g

Cholesterol: 134mg

Carbohydrate: 1.6g

Protein: 32g

Roasted Whole Ham in Apricot Sauce

Preparation time: 15 minutes

Cooking time: 2 hours

Servings: 12

Ingredients:

- 8-pound whole ham, bone-in
- 16 ounces apricot BBQ sauce
- 2 tablespoon Dijon mustard
- 1/4 cup horseradish
- Intolerances:
- Gluten-Free
- Egg-Free
- Lactose-Free

Directions:

Fill the grill hopper with apple-flavored wood pellets, power the grill on by using the control panel, select 'smoke' on the temperature dial, or set the temperature to 325°F and let it preheat for a minimum of 15 minutes.

Take a large roasting pan, line it with foil, and place ham on it.

When the grill has preheated, open the lid, place roasting pan containing ham on the grill grate, shut the grill and smoke for 1 hour and 30 minutes.

Prepare the glaze and for this, take a medium saucepan, place it over medium heat, add BBQ sauce, mustard, and horseradish, stir until mixed and cook for 5 minutes, set aside until required.

After 1 hour and 30 minutes smoking, brush ha generously with the prepared glaze and continue smoking for 30 minutes until internal temperature reaches 135°F.

Remove roasting pan from the grill, let rest for 20 minutes and then cut into slices.

Serve ham with remaining glaze.

Nutrition:

Calories: 157

Fat: 5.6g

Carbs: 4.1g

Protein: 22.1g

Awesome Pork Shoulder

Serving: 4

Prep Time: 10-15 minutes + 24 hours

Cook Time: 12 hours

Recommended Wood Type: Pecan Wood

Ingredients

- 8 pounds of pork shoulder
- For Rub
- 1 teaspoon dry mustard
- 1 teaspoon black pepper
- 1 teaspoon cumin
- 1 teaspoon oregano
- 1 teaspoon cayenne pepper
- 1/3 cup salt
- ¼ cup garlic powder
- ½ cup paprika
- 1/3 cup brown sugar
- 2/3 cup sugar

How To

Bring your pork under salted water for 18 hours

Pull the pork out from brine and let it sit for 1 hour

Rub mustard all over the pork

Take a bowl and mix all rub ingredients, rub mixture all over the meat

Wrap meat and leave it overnight

Take your drip pan and add water, cover with aluminum foil. Pre-heat your smoker to 250 degrees F

Use water fill water pan halfway through and place it over drip pan. Add wood chips to the side tray.

Transfer meat to smoker and smoke for 6 hours

Take the pork out and wrap in foil, smoke for 6 hours more at 195 degrees F

Shred and serve

Enjoy!

Nutrition Values (Per Serving)

Calories: 965

Fat: 65g

Carbohydrates: 19g

Protein: 71g

Smoked Braided Pork Loin

Prep Time: 20 Minutes

Cooking Time: 2 Hours & 55 Minutes

Servings: 8 Persons

Ingredients

- 4 to 5-pound spork loin
- Mango Chipotle Seasoning
- Olive oil
- 1 wooden kabob skewer
-

Directions

Rinse the pork loin and then, pat them dry the usage of paper towels.

To braid; make two cuts lengthwise on the loin (you need to have be having 3 related strands). Cut the loin lengthwise & all the manner thru.

Pour and rub a small amount of olive oil over the loin then, coat the beef with the beef rubs, any of your favorite.

four. Next, braid the red meat portions together after which, take a wood skewer; stick via the ends of pieces.

Preheat the grill of your wood pellets over Hi Smoke for a couple of mins. Place the coated loin over the grill & cook dinner for an hour. Once done;

turn the warmth to 275 F & maintain to prepare dinner till the internal temperature of the beef reflects 145 F. Pull off the grill after which, wrap in aluminum foil; permit the loin to rest for 12 to 15 minutes. Slice & enjoy.

Nutritional Value

891 Calories

666 Calories from Fat

74g Total Fat

33g Saturated Fat

0.5g Trans Fat

3.1g Polyunsaturated Fat

30g Monounsaturated Fat

229mg Cholesterol

513mg Sodium

900mg Potassium

1.4g Total Carbohydrates

0.4g Dietary Fiber

0.3g Sugars 52g Protein

Pork Burnt Ends

Preparation time: 15 minutes

Cooking time: 4 hours 30 minutes

Servings: 10

Ingredients:

- 4 pounds pork belly
- 4 tbsp brown sugar
- ¼ tsp cayenne pepper
- 1 tsp red pepper flakes
- ½ tsp onion powder
- ½ tsp garlic powder
- 1 tbsp paprika
- 1 tsp oregano
- 1 tbsp freshly ground black pepper
- 2 tbsp salt or to taste
- 1 tsp dried peppermint
- 2 tbsp olive oil
- ¼ cup butter

- 1 cup BBQ sauce

- 4 tbsp maple syrup

- 2 tbsp chopped fresh parsley

- Intolerances:

- Gluten-Free

- Egg-Free

Directions:

Trim pork belly of any excess fat and cut off silver skin. Cut the pork into ½ inch cubes.

To make rub, combine the sugar, cayenne, pepper flakes, onion powder, garlic, paprika, oregano, black pepper, salt, and peppermint in a mixing bowl.

Drizzle oil over the pork and season each pork cubes generously with the rub.

Preheat your grill to 205°F with lid closed for 15 minutes.

Arrange the pork chunks onto the grill grate and smoke for about 3 hours, or until the pork chunks turn dark red.

Meanwhile, combine the BBQ sauce, maple syrup and butter in an aluminum pan.

Remove the pork slices from heat and put them in the pan with the sauce.

Stir to combine.

Cover the pan tightly with aluminum foil and place it on the grill. Cook for 1 hour or until the internal temperature of the pork reaches 200°F.

Remove the pork from heat and let it sit for some minutes.

Serve and garnish with fresh chopped parsley.

Nutrition:

Calories: 477

Fat: 41.8g

Cholesterol: 58mg

Carbohydrate: 19.3g

Protein: 6.4g

Herbed Prime Rib

Serving: 4

Prep Time: 10-15 minutes

Cook Time: 4 hours

Recommended Wood Type: Pecan Wood

Ingredients

- 5 pounds prime rib
- 2 tablespoons black pepper
- ¼ cup olive oil
- 2 tablespoons salt
- Herb Paste
- ¼ cup olive oil
- 1 tablespoon fresh sage
- 1 tablespoon fresh thyme
- 1 tablespoon fresh rosemary
- 3 garlic cloves

How To

Take a blender and add herbs, blend until thoroughly combined

Take your drip pan and add water, cover with aluminum foil. Pre-heat your smoker to 225 degrees F

Use water fill water pan halfway through and place it over drip pan. Add wood chips to the side tray

Coat rib with olive oil and season it well with salt and pepper

Transfer seasoned rib to your smoker and smoke for 4 hours

Remove rib from the smoker and keep it on the side, let it cool for 30 minutes

Cut into slices and serve

Enjoy!

Nutrition Values (Per Serving)

Calories: 936

Fat: 81g

Carbohydrates: 2g

Protein: 46g

Explosive Smoky Bacon

Serving: 10

Prep Time: 20 minutes

Cook Time: 2 hours 10 minutes

Recommended Wood Type: Pecan Wood

Ingredients

- 1 pound thick-cut bacon
- 1 tablespoon BBQ spice rub
- 2 pounds bulk pork sausage
- 1 cup cheddar cheese, shredded
- 4 garlic cloves, minced
- 18 ounces BBQ sauce

How To

Take your drip pan and add water, cover with aluminum foil. Pre-heat your smoker to 225 degrees F

Use water fill water pan halfway through and place it over drip pan. Add wood chips to the side tray

Reserve about ½ a pound of your bacon for cooking later on

Lay 2 strips of your remaining bacon on a clean surface in an X formation

Alternate the horizontal and vertical bacon strips by waving them tightly in an over and under to create a lattice-like pattern

Sprinkle 1 teaspoon of BBQ rub over the woven bacon

Arrange ½ a pound of your bacon in a large-sized skillet and cook them for 10 minutes over medium-high heat

Drain the cooked slices on a kitchen towel and crumble them

Place your sausages in a large-sized re-sealable bag

While the sausages are still in the bag, roll them out to a square that has the same sized as the woven bacon

Cut off the bag from the sausage and arrange them sausage over the woven bacon

Toss away the bag

Sprinkle some crumbled bacon, green onions, cheddar cheese and garlic over the rolled sausages

Pour about ¾ bottle of your BBQ sauce over the sausage and season with some more BBQ rub

Roll up the woven bacon tightly all around the sausage, forming a loaf

Cook the bacon-sausage loaf in your smoker for about 1 and a ½ hour

Brush up the woven bacon with remaining BBQ sauce and keep smoking for about 30 minutes until the center of the loaf is no longer pink

Use an instant thermometer to check if the internal temperature is at least

165 degrees Fahrenheit

If yes, then take it out and let it rest for 30 minutes

Slice and serve!

Nutrition Values (Per Serving)

Calories: 507

Fats: 36g

Carbs: 20g

Fiber: 2g

Lovable Pork Belly

Serving: 4

Prep Time: 10-15 minutes

Cook Time: 4 hours 30 minutes

Recommended Wood Type: Pecan Wood

Ingredients

- 5 pounds of pork belly
- 1 cup dry rub
- 3 tablespoons olive oil
- For Sauce
- 2 tablespoons honey
- 3 tablespoons butter
- 1 cup BBQ sauce

How To

Take your drip pan and add water, cover with aluminum foil. Pre-heat your smoker to 250 degrees F

Add pork cubes, dry rub, olive oil into a bowl and mix well

Use water fill water pan halfway through and place it over drip pan. Add wood chips to the side tray

Transfer pork cubes to your smoker and smoke for 3 hours (covered)

Remove pork cubes from the smoker and transfer to foil pan, add honey, butter, BBQ sauce, and stir

Cover the pan with foil and transfer back to a smoker, smoke for 90 minutes more

Remove foil and smoke for 15 minutes more until the sauce thickens

Serve and enjoy!

Nutrition Values (Per Serving)

Calories: 1164

Fat: 68g

Carbohydrates: 12g

Protein: 104g

Lemon Pepper Pork Tenderloin

Preparation time: 20 minutes

Cooking time: 20 minutes

Servings: 6

Ingredients:

- 2 pounds pork tenderloin, fat trimmed
- For the Marinade:
- ½ teaspoon minced garlic
- 2 lemons, zested
- 1 teaspoon minced parsley
- 1/2 teaspoon salt
- 1/4 teaspoon ground black pepper
- 1 teaspoon lemon juice
- 2 tablespoons olive oil
- Intolerances:
- Gluten-Free
- Egg-Free
- Lactose-Free

Directions:

Prepare the marinade and for this, take a small bowl, place all ingredients in it and whisk until combined.

Take a large plastic bag, pour marinade in it, add pork tenderloin, seal the bag, turn it upside down to coat the pork and let it marinate for a minimum of 2 hours in the refrigerator.

Fill the grill hopper with apple-flavored wood pellets, power the grill on by using the control panel, select 'smoke' on the temperature dial, or set the temperature to 375°F and let it preheat for a minimum of 15 minutes.

When the grill has preheated, open the lid, place pork tenderloin on the grill grate, shut the grill and smoke for 20 minutes until internal temperature reaches 145°F, turning pork halfway.

When done, transfer pork to a cutting board, let it rest for 10 minutes, then cut it into slices and serve.

Nutrition:

Calories: 288

Fat: 16.6g

Carbs: 6.2g

Protein: 26.4g

Smoked Pork Ribs

Prep Time: 20 Minutes

Cooking Time: 6 Hours & 20

Minutes Servings: 6 Persons

Ingredients

- 3 racks baby back ribs
- 1 ½ tablespoon mustard
- BBQ Rub, any of your favorite
- 1 ½ tablespoon maple syrup
- ½ cup apple juice
- Coarse salt
- For Glaze
- 1 cup ketchup
- ½ cup maple syrup
- 3 tablespoons hot sauce
- 1 teaspoon pepper
- 3 tablespoons vinegar
- ½ cup mustard

Directions

Rinse the ribs & then, patting them dry the usage of a paper towel. Score the silver skin (membrane) at the concave side of the ribs; peel it off using a paper towel. Generously season the ribs with salt after which, permit the brine to dry for an hour.

Combine the apple juice with maple syrup and mustard in a sprig bottle. Combine the whole glaze ingredients together in a medium sized bowl; set the aggregate aside till equipped to use.

three. Preheat your pellet grill with excessive smoke. Once you've got brined the ribs have for one hour; spritz them with the organized aggregate within the spray bottle. Cover the ribs absolutely with the organized rub & put them in a smoker; cook dinner for three hours. Once done; spread the glaze on pinnacle of the ribs & cover them in an aluminum foil; continue to smoke for 2 greater hours. Get rid of the foil & prepare dinner for an hour; don 't neglect to spread a few more glaze on pinnacle of the meat. Serve warm and enjoy.

Nutritional Value

595 Calories, 323 Calories from Fat

36g Total Fat, 42g Protein

13g Saturated Fat, 0.3g Trans Fat

5.9g Polyunsaturated Fat

15g Monounsaturated Fat

146mg Cholesterol

719mg Sodium

597mg Potassium

24g Total Carbohydrates

0.9g Dietary Fiber

19g Sugars

CPSIA information can be obtained
at www.ICGtesting.com
Printed in the USA
BVHW090324220621
610126BV00012B/3035